First published by Accidental Publishing 2020

Cataloguing-in-Publication entry is available from the National Library of Australia
http://catalogue.nla.gov.au

ISBN 978-1-9259000-0-2 (paperback)
Memoir / Literary Collection
Dewey Number 928

Typeset in 10 pt Athleas Regular
Printed and bound by Ingram

Cover image and artwork by Lauren Starr Photographic Artist
www.laurenstarr.com.au

Accidental Publishing
An imprint of Of The World Books
PO Box 8070 Bendigo South LPO VIC 3550
Australia
www.oftheworldbooks.com

Mother

Memories, moments & stories

CONTENTS

FOREWORD

If there's a topic that literature loves, it's mothers. From the anxious and hysterical Mrs Bennet in *Pride and Prejudice*, back to the awesomely fearful Medea of Greek tragedy, and forward to Patrick White's destructive matriarch Elizabeth Hunter in *The Eye of the Storm*, mothers inspire beautiful (if disturbing) fiction.

Fuelling some of that rich creativity are myths and even clichés about women, their places in society and in the home. So, because Bendigo Writers Festival's Big Bookmark event was planned to fall on Mother's Day in 2020, we decided it was the perfect opportunity to get real about mothers.

We put out a call for contributions, for Central Victorians to tell us about their mothers. We received many more offers than we could include in this small book, and the emotion that rippled through the writing was so intense, it has made it very clear this matters to people. To have an opportunity to remember, to consider, to honour mothers has opened up such a store of memories, we were overwhelmed with the response.

This collection contains humour and sadness. Ageing is now, fortunately, much less of a taboo topic, so to read about the loss that many people experience even before the death of their mother is powerful. While there is just one story that takes us to difficult places – when the mother-child relationship is broken – these stories underline the strength so many people feel in the maternal bond. It gives us an opportunity to consider not only what is behind that strength, but also how circumstances within families and within communities are central to how relationships are built.

I love this collection, in all its variety, colour and emotion. Thankyou to all the contributors and to Amy Doak, who, once more, has been so supportive of Central Victorian writing.

I could cite so many memorable moments described here, that surprised and delighted me, some so moving it brought tears to my eyes. But I'll mention just one, which I think underlines why the publication of this book is so rewarding. It comes from Rodney Carter's tribute to his mother Fay, who, as a Dja Dja Wurrung child growing up in Bendigo, would have to stand at the back of a shop until the non-Indigenous women had been served.

"Your grandmother taught you that when you were picked on, not to worry," Rodney recalls his mother telling him, "because one day they would understand who you are and treat you better."

This is a book that might just help us understand who these women are, and maybe that will also help us to treat each other better.

- Rosemary Sorensen
(Director, Bendigo Writers Festival)

FAY PRISCILLA CARTER
by Rodney Carter

Mother, if the community is your children you have done so much to nurture them.

You were born on the veranda of a rural hospital because your mother was not allowed to share in a ward with the other women. You lived your early life in a hut at a floodplain by the banks of a river. Your grandmother taught you that when you were picked upon, not to worry, because one day they would understand who you are and treat you better. You had to stand at the back wall of a shop until everyone else was served and then it was your turn. You have shared so many of your memories with me, and sometimes with tears in your eyes because of your sadness, but you have given me your wisdom, your tolerance and your love. You speak of your life with happiness, and tell us to be thankful for being at all, understanding that our existence is right and proper because the old people before us were beautiful people.

Oh, mother why do you love so much, why do you care for all of your community children so dearly? Is it because of the words of your grandmother when she said that one day they will understand us? Your own nurture you say was beautiful and so for me you have made mine beautiful. You are precious and it is comforting to seek your hug, feel your hug, be held in your arms gently and firmly. Your presence is warming, it casts a shadow we cannot see that shades us all from the harshness of a world that has challenged you most of your life. You have taught me without knowing, as I have watched from near and far seeing you always walking proud, working tirelessly for us and community.

When I was a child, you took me to many athletics events. A special one was the Highland Games at Maryborough, when I ran the 400m and came second. I always tried my best, and now I know it was always for you, as you were always there watching, but in your eyes really I came first. You believed the best in everyone. From the early days of your work, you have given your best. I never recall a day that you were not well enough to work. Every day you would rise in our home before all others and prepare a morning meal. You would ensure we were always fed and well clothed so we could enter the world prepared, as you had been warned and learnt that the world can judge us harshly if we were not to the standards expected. You had seen what happened to other families if this was not done.

Your journey of work and caring for others led you to social service and I recall the pride you had in yourself when you achieved a Diploma of Social Work, and now you were going to spend a large part of your life in

Aboriginal Affairs to help our people like you had never before. These years took you eventually to aged care, because our Elders needed a care they had not needed before. Even while our society modernised and enjoyed many improvements, you saw how the most important people in our families fell by the wayside, and how families became fractured, leaving older people in need of proper, personalised care.

When you ceased employment you never ceased your work, you never stopped caring and now with your life's experiences you have continued to contribute. When we were punished as a people for just talking our language always broke your heart and saddened you. Now you were to ensure others would see the true beauty in our culture, through leadership, art, song, dance and spoken word in Dja Dja Wurrung language. Making your voice heard through negotiations with the State of Victoria, at public events, in crafting cultural adornments, your presence was calming. Your presence has power and gives confidence to others that your Ancestors you love so dearly are resting in a better place with smiles upon their faces.

I am honoured to be your child, and that we have shared life's joys and struggles together, and I couldn't have been any more fortunate than to be with you in your life to see you love and care for all.

Rodney Carter

THIS MAVEN WAS A FLIPPER

by Dawn Rasmussen

One of my earliest memories is of my mum on all fours polishing the lino in the little hallway from the back door and into the kitchen of our ten-square housing commission house.

As I looked at those skinny legs sticking out from a pair of homemade striped pink shorts, I made a vow to my eight-year-old self – I was never, ever going to do that floor polishing caper.

In the late 1950s our small town was a refugee stronghold, and this included mum. As a single mother of two children, she had left grandma and grandpa's house in Melbourne and set up as a housekeeper for a chap who had four children.

Before too long this 'Brady Bunch', all of similar ages, called her mum, and as Loretta Lynn would sing around that era, 'One's on the way', was also a reality for mum.

This event was too much for the grandparents; all contact ceased and the will was rewritten.

I asked her recently how she managed to go from a housing commission renter to a property owner in about 12 years, with eight kids and a wilting partner.

This is the amazing tale she told me.

When the new baby was born, Mum still didn't know too many people in town. While she was in hospital, the nursing sister said to Mrs Parkinson, who lived up the end of the housing commission street and also had just delivered a new baby, to go along to mum's room as she could probably do with someone to talk to. She had not had one visitor, not even the 'father'.

Mum and Mrs P. hit it off straight away.

Mum was a bit worried that the housing commission house was going to burst at the seams with so many of us, and Mrs P. told her about a project her builder husband was working on. He was redeveloping a property and needed a few old railway houses moved off the land.

Mum just laughed and said she couldn't afford one house let alone two.

Mrs P. persisted and said the houses were free as they were in the way. If mum could get them moved on to some cheap house block and do them up, they would become a good little earner from the rent. Mum just shrugged and said it was a nice pipedream.

In the meantime, the in-laws visited and mum's father-in-law asked for the return of the ten pounds he had lent them about five years earlier. Dad was handing the money over when his mother saw what was happening and she flew into an almighty rage.

"Arch, how dare you take that money? They have eight mouths to feed. Give him back the ten pound note immediately, take that fat roll out of your pocket, and give them a hundred pounds more on top of that. Straight away," Millie said.

Mum knew what to do with some of that money, and went and bought cheap land with all services on the edge of town.

She knew of a local Spanish chap who was a handyman builder, and went to see his wife to make sure everyone knew it was a business arrangement and that mum would pay him by the hour for the work that would need doing.

The first house was a bit of a disaster. The chimney for the heater was in the wrong place, which meant the chimney bricks had to be dismantled, cleaned, and then the chimney rebuilt.

There were several other seemingly insurmountable problems before the house could be rented, until mum realised that the real estate agent, with only four kids and no home of his own, was so jealous of mum making a success of the relocated house, that he kept finding faults, just because he could. Mum took the house out of his hands and did private rentals after that.

Everything settled down.

Dad had really got into the spirit of moving houses and soon approached a landowner from their church and persuaded him to part with a lazy corner of his property, where he ran prized Hereford cattle. Dad wouldn't be a bother, he promised him.

So mum and dad, with the help of an old bloke dad knew, moved another house, cut in half and transported on an old two-ton truck, for their own use.

Then with a fair portion of her nest egg still intact, mum decided to relocate the second little railway house. The Spanish builder was on board, and it was a much easier project this time around.

After the third house was moved, remodelled and a renter settled in, the Spanish chap said to mum, “I’m going back to Spain with my family. We have saved all the money we earned doing your building and renovations, and we will be able to live like kings from here on. Why don’t you bring the kids and make a new life too?”

Being a Sagittarius, mum did give it quite a lot of thought, as new places and faces were always her thing, but she decided against it. All the kids were now in school and life seemed to be on the up for this early adopter of the house flipper concept.

THE ART OF KNITTING

by Helen Hickson

My mum loved to knit and crochet. She could knit anywhere and at anytime including while she was watching TV, at the football and while we were in the car (not while she was driving of course). We never ceased to be embarrassed about her knitting in public places, like at the cinema or the doctor's waiting room.

My mum was born in 1947 and died in 2009 after a short encounter with cancer. I often think about Mum when I see the latest yarn bombing creations. She would have loved it.

Mum was a great knitter. She enjoyed making jumpers with intricate and colourful patterns and she desperately wanted her children to embrace the hand-knitted jumpers, but we never did. They were too scratchy, too daggy, never quite right and not the brand names that our friends wore.

Mum was a creator. She soon progressed from jumpers and cardigans to knitted crafts. She sometimes followed patterns but would often free-style and adapt patterns to suit the occasion. I remember when I got married it was expected to give each guest a gift of bomboniere and Mum tried out several patterns of crochet doilies that were soaked in starch and sugar syrup until they went stiff and formed nests that were then filled with sugared almonds. She made over a hundred of these to give one to each wedding guest.

Then Mum discovered knitted toys and dolls. Her favourite designer was Jean Greenhowe and she had all her pattern books. She made clowns that were embellished in the recipient's favourite football team colours, teddies, the Topsy Turvy Doll, the Cinderella Doll and even the occasional golliwog. There were mini Christmas stockings, knitted Christmas decorations and one year she made a knitted nativity scene and Dad knocked up a manger with wood, sticks and straw. It was spectacular and as I got older, I began to appreciate the unique, individuality of hand-made items.

After my mum died, my sister and I collected two huge garbage bags full of knitted dolls and over the years we have handed them out to family and friends as mum would have done.

For centuries, women have used yarn not only to knit or weave clothing and blankets but also to introduce colour and texture into the home. My grandmother knitted elaborate tea cosies that were used to keep tea warm and introduce colour and individuality to the kitchen table.

As the art of knitting and crochet spread outside the family home and hit the streets the phenomenon known as yarn bombing emerged. Usually (but not always) created by women, yarn bombing is a type of street art that involves wrapping objects in crochet or knitted works. Some of the earliest examples of public yarn bombing date back to 2002, although the term didn't catch on until 2005. Like graffiti, yarn bombing is usually installed by stealth in the dark of night – guerrilla style – and is designed to draw attention and to get people talking. While graffiti is usually dominated by men, yarn bombing is more feminine with matronly, maternal gestures of wrapping something cold in a warm blanket. The motivation for yarn bombing is to bring fun, colour and life to a community space. All over the world, statues are dressed with colourful socks, a scarf or a warm woollen vest, and bike racks, bridges and even trees have received a warm wrap to see them through the cold winter months. You can even study yarn bombing at university and there is now an International Yarn Bombing Day on 11 June.

Yarn bombing is not without its critics. Utilitarian types may struggle to see the point of it, and some people see yarn bombing in public places as a kind of vandalism. Concerns have been expressed about the impact to trees, birds and insects when a tree is covered with acrylic fibres.

In Bendigo, yarn bombing has been around for a while and fits in with the vibrant arts community. Colourful yarns adorn bridges, trees and the famous crochet-covered Talking Tram. Bendigo yarn bombers have a no-name, no-face policy and the anonymity adds to the mystique.

As I travel around Australia, I notice that yarn bombing is installed in many towns, both rural and urban. Shepparton's Motor Museum has a yarn-bombed BMX bike and rider covered in colourful knitted squares.

The pièce de résistance was the discovery of a special yarn bombed couch in Eden, NSW. The visitor's centre proudly displayed the couch that has been covered with a collection of Jean Greenhowe's knitted dolls and it was used as a fund-raiser for the local hospital. As I sat there, I thought of my Mum. She would have loved this couch and she would probably have convinced Dad that we should do this at home. She would love yarn bombing and would love the idea of installing knitted art in the dark of night. I can hear her chuckle at the critics and complaints.

NANCIE HESSE LUND
by Elizabeth Beck

On Easter Sunday 2001, at 7am, the phone rang. It was my sister, who said, "I think you should come as Mum has deteriorated overnight".

I flew out that morning from Perth, and mid-flight, something made me take off the headphones. I felt Mum leave our earthly existence. At that time my sister was holding Mum's hand at her bedside and she told Mum I was on my way from Perth. Mum squeezed my sister's hand and peacefully slipped away.

April holds many anniversaries in my family. Mum's Dad's birthday was 15 April; Mum and Dad's wedding was 20 April, 1935; Mum's sister's untimely death was 25 April 1938; and my divorce was 21 April, 1989.

Now it was up to me to give my last gift to Mum – a eulogy at her funeral service.

Born 15 July, 1913, six years after her only sibling, Mum was considered somewhat of an afterthought. She always felt she was in the shadow of her tall, confident, talented sister Jean, who was a champion rower. Next door to her family home, only four months older than Mum, was Mum's lifelong friend Isabel. Mum envied Isa's dark curls, but they were inseparable.

As a small child Mum was hospitalized for many weeks with a severe case of diphtheria. They painted her throat with a feather dipped in gentian violet, which was the treatment back then.

Mum's childhood home was set in a lovely Victorian era garden that was divided into garden rooms. She had a wonderful life-size playhouse, which had a gabled roof, iron lace along the porch and was beautifully decorated by my artisan painter and decorator grandfather. The far yard contained poultry, which my grandmother fattened for special festive occasions. Peppercorn trees screened the back fence from the adjacent railway line. My grandmother had a heart of gold, as she would feed weary travellers who rested in a pavilion at the lake and gardens opposite the family home. She also made clothes for the orphaned babies at St. Luke's toddler's home. I'm sure these gestures had a great influence on my mother's generosity.

When Mum was little the Chinese vegetable man called each week with fresh vegetables and he always brought Mum a little bag of lollies and on special occasions like birthday and Christmas a special gift. One such gift I donated to the Bendigo Chinese museum. It is a little padded basket containing a porcelain teapot.

Although it was a distance from her home, Mum rode her bike or caught the tram to Gravel Hill primary school. She then went to Bendigo High School, and later she was a student teacher at Camp Hill primary school. After twelve months a student teacher would go on to teacher's college before being sent to rural or remote small schools. My grandmother was having none of that, so she organized for Mum to work in the Haberdashery Department of Myer in Bendigo.

During the depression years employment was scarce and Mum recalls working one week on and interchanging with another for her one week off. They were paid wages of two and six pence per week. Mum's work colleague Nell Wilson became another of her lifelong friends.

At 16 she had a form of cancer in her jawbone requiring her to have all her teeth extracted and replaced with dentures. This was a common practice in those days. In her youth Mum played tennis at what was then known as 'Wilkie Park', which is now a sporting venue at the Northern end of Lake Weeroona.

Dad was sent to Bendigo as a mechanical engineer to set up the machinery for a Swiss company, Hanro Knitting Mills. A new lad in town, he caught Mum's eye. They were married in Forest St. Methodist Church on 20 April (Easter Saturday) 1935. They honeymooned in Marysville, then moved into a brand new Californian bungalow built by Axel Anderson at 50 Lucan St, Bendigo. This was to be their residence for the next 28 years. Here Mum honed her cookery skills. She was a great homemaker delighting in exploring new recipes making beautiful cakes, biscuits, slices, preserves and interesting meals. Many of her ideas came from the *Woman's Weekly*, which she purchased each Friday from Hampton's newsagency in Charing Cross.

She always said her war efforts were giving birth to three baby girls, supporting Dad with his war fund-raising efforts and hosting American GIs on R+R leave from the Pacific. These USA service men had not had their boots off in months. They were brought to Bendigo by train, marched down the centre of the road and a number would be called and they had to file off either left or right to be billeted with a family. We never knew the service men's real names or much about their personal lives, or if they even survived the war years.

Our home had block-out blinds and an air raid shelter Dad had dug into the back yard as the Ordnance factory was only one mile away. Petrol and food were rationed, but Mum had extra petrol rations as I was a sick baby and she had to come to the hospital several times a day.

In many ways Mum was a modern lady. She gained her driver's licence at 18 and was always independent with her own car. This became a personal taxi with driver for my grandparents and elderly family members.

Very supportive of education, and particularly for girls, Mum always sourced out the best environments for our learning. She always held positions on our school mother's clubs, school advisory councils and church guilds. She worked tirelessly with fundraising efforts, particularly when our local church was burnt by an arsonist. A small group from the church set up catering to raise the money for rebuilding the church, a new hall and amenities. Mum really thrived through these efforts.

But there was also a fun side to Mum. During the 1950s she joined in the latest craze of square dancing. One night a week she would head off with her basket containing supper and a thermos flask to dance away the night. Then there were the winter balls that mum and Dad attended. The Mayoral Ball, the Masonic Ball and the Return Ball. It was exciting to see Mum dressed up in her beautiful ball gowns, silver dancing shoes, and fur complete with corsage. It also meant that us girls could have a sleepover at neighbours' homes. Mum once performed in a stage musical at the Eaglehawk Town Hall with a group of women from the West Methodist fellowship.

Here's what my mother gave to her three daughters: sincerity, good grace, respect for security and education, good manners. She said to me that she had lived a good life exceeding all expectations. She quietly slipped away just three months short of her 88th birthday. Fond memories Mum, and I miss you.

A MODERN MOTHER

by Nat Jane

In the photograph you are sitting on the front veranda of our idyllic country home with a cup of tea in your hand. A fox terrier is seated in front of you, gazing up at you, awaiting your next move. You frequently sit here in the bright morning light and on this day, one of your adoring children has snapped this picture. Whilst at school, I would think of you sitting on the veranda. Alone. No-one for miles around. A town girl now living in such acute isolation. You came here when you were 30 years old and it will be another 13 years before you are back in town, enjoying a modicum of independence in your work at the hospital. Having coffee with friends.

Four years before you leave the farm, your daughters have moved away. I know you would have wept all the way home from Melbourne the day you, my lovely family, dropped me off at a university residential college. Every February, almost 30 years later, I look at the newly-arrived first year students who are living on campus and think of their mothers, living far away, weeping silently on the return trip from universities across the country. Being chastised for being silly by their husbands.

I try and make up for anything I feel you may have missed during these lonely, quiet years on the farm. I replace your bargain makeup from the sale bin with YSL and Dior. I buy you things that I know you will love and have never bought for yourself. You tell me off for spending so much money, but I see the joy in your eyes and would happily have spent twice as much (and probably will next year!).

I hear you making the peace, keeping the peace. Tolerating disrespect for the sake of peace. I witness you not standing up for yourself, for to do so would be to invite further argument, so you quietly absorb the comments. I see now what that has done to you. It's made you nervous and uncertain, constantly seeking approval. I sometimes catch myself reacting the same way and I wish you had shown me how to stand tall and not let disparaging comments go without a retort. To not feel diminished.

I marvel at how you still see me as child. You watch me type on the computer keyboard marvelling at my speed and accuracy. For a moment I feel like a proud child. Then I remember that I am over 50 years old and have 20 years of administration experience. I tell you that I've changed the garden tap washers or have painted a wall and you say that I can turn my hand to anything. I explain that it's all because of online instructional videos. I love that you now watch many of these videos and have learnt to crochet.

I remember fondly how old-fashioned some of your ideas were when I was a teenager, especially now when I think of you as a thoroughly modern woman, seventy plus years young. I remember when you discussed potential 21st birthday gifts for me with my aunts and grandparents. Linen and Cristal d'Arques glasses! It all seemed a bit out of character for me, a leather-jacket-clad Sex Pistols fan. Your mother taught you to be a good mother, have a clean house and well-mannered children. Your own children taught you that you could exercise some choices in what you wore and what music you listened to.

I return to visit you and dad and am instantly relieved of the burden of being an adult. I am a child. And you are a mother again. You enjoy asking me if I want dessert. You are on your feet and half way to the fridge before I answer. We play out our roles from years ago in a subconscious act of remembrance or nostalgia. Maybe it's our safe place. These were significant roles for both of us and we enjoy replaying them for a while.

I've loved watching you grow and am so pleased that you were young and healthy enough to taste a few of the freedoms and choices that I take for granted. Ceramics classes, line dancing, trips to Tamworth with girlfriends, overseas trips, eating Thai food! Your service certificate from the Hospital proudly hanging on the wall. You could never have imagined the life your daughters and son have had. Broken relationships, resigning from various workplaces, undertaking new jobs. You shake your head and think we are crazy, but I observed you coming around. You seemed quite old-fashioned as a 1980s wife and mother and in 2020 you are a modern 70-something with bright pink nail polish and a polite strength. You have acquired the art of speaking your mind. It has been truly marvellous to watch you grow within yourself and for yourself.

NO ROYAL BLOODLINES
by Karen Lee Mills

No royal blood lines,
Or any claim to fame,
Born to a railway man,
His wife a kitchen maid.

Noelene was the first born,
Brothers who were larrikins,
Never far from trouble,
One sister, a dear friend for life.

A storyteller in her own right,
Many hardships overcome,
Secret sacrifices willingly made for others,
She would never dare tell.

Sharing her gifts and talents,
Stretching a meal to feed unexpected guests,
Knitting baby clothes or toys for those in need,
Sewing all kinds of things, never too hard a task.

Mum loves to sit and read a book,
Sharing a cuppa with her friends,

Playing cards till late at night,
Until another day begins or ends.

Let me whisper your praise,
You have taught me many things,
How to read, write and draw,
How to sew, knit and cook.

The most important thing you have taught me,
Is how to be a mother,
You have demonstrated patience and kindness,
Sharing love to one and another.

My mother is a humble lady,
She is so precious to me,
I am thankful for the time we spend,
Knowing one day it will all come to an end.

You are more than royalty to me,
You are an amazing mother,
I love you dearly,
I am blessed to call you, Mum.

LINES OF BLOOD & WATER & STONE

by T.S.F Dowling

This fallible life bathed in forgiveness because of you. my mother.

Wild

Stories float
memories of when
you wandered the bush for wild
flowers, plucked a red-
robed girl in a bluish wilderness
from fairytales
you sang me.

Threat

Mother, on a quickening
breeze your breath carries
urgency, a tone
snapped as a life-
line towards our wandering.

Just seven years old, with younger
sister, I wind around bitumen, paddock,
and over barbed
wire away from you
to pick pinecones like crowns

near the train tracks. Above us,
wisha-whisper through a mosaic
of light and bark, needles
green as their scent, the rustle
of dead stuff underfoot.   A man makes

his way along the tracks,
picking up papers. Your voice –
a shotgun crack, an echo, a sonar
bouncing off tree trunk and threat. We
turn to home, fear of your anger

a fist in my gut. Your frame
leans over balustrade, arm salutes
air, instils in me a warning,
a marker,
a lighthouse beam.

Resumed

Under the middle-weight
of six children, your muscle

sagged, gravity-fed
our appetites. Pressure
cooking (lashings of it) for tongues
caught in the criss-crossfire
of fine sliced cutlery, posturing
moments En Garde!

My lazy locks, severed
in a pony tail, followed our cavalry
formation along corridors to bathroom,
three-a-tub, teeth checked, backs scrubbed,
PJed, prayered, then one-by-one served
bed, chin-tucked with a slather
of lightening kisses to forehead,
story-less.

Ten minutes into black, I pitch
a tent, a torch that picks fine
black 'o's of Goldy Locks and burly
'b's of bears bellowing
"Who's this sleeping in MY bed?"

Thirty years in the meantime story
continuum – ringing

Adventists are at the door the phone
is shouting obscenities at the TV
        the rope-able children are performing the dog

is having words with the neighbour's adopted
possum the washing machine screams
tuning the abandoned hoover.
And in someone else's bed, a half-read
book lies face-down, waiting
for its yellowing
pages to be
resumed.

Leave

Regiments get into the blood (for better
or worse), could string you up, till you take
leave. Your frown-lines followed
your mother's lead to dances and shows,
learned couture from her,
shoes, gloves, lipstick, immaculate; your eyes
misted as Swan Lake cut from the lid
of a chocolate-box. Framed, the scene hangs
in my hallway still. Swirls of past (and I)
grow from, into
you, Mother.

Mum's Gloves

We watch your hands
anticipate the soft cloth innards
flocked in a nest of midnight shimmer

wrist-stitched in mother-of-pearl buttons,
our baby full-moon faces beaming
till you leave us, after a few quick pecks,
engine purring into night.

We peel back covers,
pick top drawer pockets,
arms burrowing into each slim cave;
fingers unfurl wings,
a wave not quite regal, till
over-elbows-elegant, we're
off to the ball.

Flowers of Stone

Over shoulder boulder holders –
the name we give to independence
rather than 'training' to gain a bra,
proof bosoms blossom like flowers of stone
(to feed the mouths and grow the bones),
these days swing on the hinge of childhood, free
skirted daisy days, picking one, two, stringing a garland
for crowns or neck-lines, slitting stalks or hem-lines
(spark slutty talk, and sniggering behind the shed);
dress-up days lead us along forked paths, tongues
pressed to movie star posters or hands
we lick like postage stamps, saliva frothing round
the edges, we're mad as a top dog on glue,

or a hot bitch's juicy stories whispered
with the sacred sun on our silky manes
clutched in a pony tail, a tissue, we all fall down
clasping grass seeds and dandelion puffs
that float like fairy-floss, these chasing days
all hot breath and bothered like a steam train escaping
while kettle's heated to boiling inside, its spout sprouting
full-o-beans and a means to an end or to begin again each day,
every day's a play day, a wait and see
or jump and splash day, where blood gashes
from between legs or a head wound day,
when running past the metal swing that swings
and cuts and wounds, while our baby brother
sucks the milk dregs of your affection, Mother,
and your eyes pale as a frosted stare,
not a spare red cent in your bone shoulder-strapped day,
then our bags are packed and out we go,
all preened and prepped like a comb
carefully pulled through your straw hair, sprayed
and displayed, before you disparaged and we raged and raged,
these days are days
we couldn't
do without, have done
without you.

A Headlight

When I was ill, for months in hospital, you rang me

every night, reminded me God was near, you were there. You were always there. Years passed. Your independence progressed. Apart from dinner with friends, or a tour with Dad, you worked and worked, Mother; never stopped. My father's business was making pies (in the shop and the sky); you supported each calculated week, selling (and buying) food. Your frugal nous earned you much, cost us more. Your heart lurched, attacked in the small hours, attempted to retire you. I visited and you pottered from room to room, gave me 15 minutes of your time to sit, have a cuppa and afternoon tea, tell me how you worried about your sons, if they could settle down, cope with life, support themselves like you. We girls would be alright, it was understood, a given, unspoken, like the unspeakable you carried, released in nightmares . . .

Bolt-upright screaming, gasping . . . as if a hand across your mouth, whiff of alcohol, a tree-trunk leg forcing yours apart . . . no breath . . . a headlight flashes, frees you . . . until . . .
Over and over, late home from work, my father finds you glass-eyed, shivering . . .

Dad tells us your story . . . shards of past as if it is still happening from when you were first married . . . of that fateful night before he came into your life . . . You sleep with the hall-light flooding till dawn. So we won't be scared, you tell us . . .

But I am scared, for you, for me, when I am much older. They caught your attacker. Your father dropped the charges, said enough's enough. My father could only comfort you later, could hardly hold you.

Fear and control are insidious; assert themselves throughout these interim years. They fight your body, your mind; niggle at tasks undone.

Threads

My mother's clothes
are threaded with tiny holes
that map disintegration

slowly. She holds a needle
between the forefinger & thumb
of her right hand to mend

my father's worn knees
and ripped pockets.
She attempts to dispel

tremors at intervals, while silver
wefts & weaves, in & out,
closing gaps, patching

his work days back together

(with King Gee taupes & bakers' whites)
as her own appear to thin.

They sit by a flame
blue as flesh, warding off colds, flu
& other ailments, sure of

airborne dangers, drawn to
the fire's heart. They lean on
cushions flat as deflated tyres,

buffering hips & spines,
close to the bone. My mother
is armed against wear

for years to come.
Her wicker basket holds spare
darning needles, buttons,

an army of spools carrying
ten thousand feet of cotton,
her usefulness intact.

Switch

You taught me to sew, an essential skill for
a girl to have; would land me work, save me
money. Like typing. Ah, what work!

Carefully placed stitches and words
bind identities we wear
and switch as if changing outfits. We resist
the ephemeral between
habit and hesitancy.

Thrift

They're moving house.
Fifty-five odd years together
rounds down to these few weeks.

Every decision, a life-time
trigger: what to keep, to lose?

Styrofoam boxes
hold glass, crystal, fine-bone
tea sets, platters, vases.

Their etched beauty,
feathered with age,
wrapped in the local rag.

She cuts the buttons off old shirts,
anticipates future fastenings.

He ogles Astair and Rogers,
rewinds and 'does-over'

their wall to ceiling dance. He makes

dinner, prepped hours before,
while she's glued to the nightly news:

more miners buried, a prem baby saved,
a cost to visit the doctor, higher
priced fuel, all claw at her conscience –

we've got to be careful!
He comes in, sits beside her,

brings biscuits, dip, pre-dinner drinks:
one red, one white with soda.

Their program occupies just
twenty minutes of its hour. Amongst ads,
a child lost at the train station

stirs her tears. Her white fizz flattens.
A crescent moon winks in his shiraz.

The hoot of the night express
echoes through the lounge.

She undresses by the fire.
He snores before bed.
Soon the house will wake without them.

Water Lines

- Bath

Swathed in this
silk-filled vessel,
her inhibitions dissolve –
an osmosis of return.
Flesh remembers fluidity
in-utero, cast-iron lined.

- Swamp

Her womb leaks like tears
of a wound that won't heal,
its octogenarian lining
sheer as cloud, marbled
beyond making.
Blood swamps the parched years,
migrates to ground.

- Rain

She is relearning the first
language of herself, taking in
the drops that spatter
her lips cheeks neck stretched
to the heavens. She mouths

the taste, traces her damp skin
as if scrawling the lines
of a song forgotten.

A Vision

We sit in the garden,
where an arc of rain sprinkles across
us perched in upright recliners.

We sip tea, dribble biscuits,
while birds teach us
their speech and songs, a glossary

of urgent industry
in thickets, hidden nests, flight,
or pecking bravado inches from her hand.

Hear their chittering? *chip twitter*
whoop See their busyness
from bush to branch, tree-top to gutter.

Droplets dot our delight, her face
a vision of a virgin, pure peace, a smile
crinkling intermittent sighs.

These Reductions

Her blush reappears
in twilight sky – over and over
on the drive home.
And I am not alone

yet. Her hands are a wilderness
of brown spots and veins,
cold with waiting
for the frost before dawn.

Her fingers mime grasp,
overhang mine.
Each ridged nail reveals
a sliver of moon.

She plucks tissues
(like white-winged creatures)
from the earth of her lap.
She bundles them close,

dabs at crumbs,
missing her mouth. Her timbre,
retuned from a magpie's, fades
through breath and air.

Tears make no noise

or fuss, their leaves
brighten then fall
across the years.

Years elusive as blinking
now counted in hours
spent together. Those years
when I was never

alone, she was
practising these reductions.
Her form shadowing
unwritten galaxies.

Caretaker

You left me in the quiet breath
of morning. Frost formed crystals
on Lake Johanna, the Persian hue of dawn

bloomed over Mount Alexander,
ice cloaked the winter-green hills
as I drove to your bedside.

Day grew to noise, bird chatter
bursting hollow in the Sun's still path;
phones and clocks urgent as prayers unanswered.

You wrap me in the Guildford twilight
of storm clouds edged blue,
where Cockatoos skim trees

bathed in light,
to settle in paddocks like snow.
Your spirit blows through my bones.

You are the fabric of our family,
woven into us – each thread,
a careful tenderness.

You capture me in a drift
of wattle, the crack of bark underfoot,
frog-song from the bush dam.

Your hair, feather-soft,
eyes green as moss on sandstone,
your lips alight with horizon.

Our faces speak
your silence, your life-blood
through our veins, sure as

you held me, firm and forgiving,
and felt for a pulse. You showed me
how a heart works. How to grasp
life's elusive dignity

for the time this earth allows,
and when to watch as love lets go.

Your voice, your presence, your effort,
darling Mother, rise from hidden springs,
giver of my life, caretaker of my heart . . .

i.m. VF

BLOODLINES
by Joan Strack O'Brien

My mother's story has never been told
She instead carried with her
The stories of the mothers who
Came before her
Over centuries
And passed a single story down
From mother to mother
Through their bloodlines to
My mother's heart
Her mind
And her soul

I only wanted sons
To relieve my unborn daughters
Of the burden of this story
And the weight of living a life
That is not your own
But my sons were never
Birthed
And my daughters
Live their lives unencumbered
By their bloodlines
Allowing my daughters
To freely love
My mother's heart
Her mind
And her soul

QUESTIONS

There are questions that I have
Never dared to ask my mother
While she is alive
Or know the answers to
When she is gone

I wonder if
She has ever been asked
These questions
Or if they have floated
Through the air around her
For an infinite number of moments
Waiting to be beckoned
Yet never found
By those of us
Who didn't search carefully enough

There are questions that
My mother has never dared to ask
Of Herself
To which neither she nor I
Will ever know the answers

HERE & THERE
by Jacqueline Anne Sheridan

If you need to let go, you can let go. I'm here."

Carving a heart with my hands in the still waters of Lake Taupo, I am miles away from her, yet in this moment of unsullied intimacy, there is little to separate us. And perhaps even less than I think.

Looking back, I'm not sure if I initiated this encounter, or if I was simply responding to her. She was losing her footing in this world and our roles had long ago reversed, as Daughter now cared for Mother. But in these final moments, perhaps she was already crossing the threshold, inhabiting enough of the next world to once again be able to reach out to me. Perhaps what seemed to be my thought, my impulse, was actually hers, nudging my heart to tune in, to grant me the only kind of goodbye I would have the chance to give.

A beloved friend later suggested that the whole circumstance of my being away on retreat, surrounded by people of my soul-tribe, might have been her final mother-love offering, ensuring that I was deeply, heartfully held by them in the moment of shattering loss. That would be so like Mum.

But when the call came from my brother later that

day to tell me that she had gone, any enlightened idea of my distance from her being a gift was entirely swallowed in darkness. I was left drowning in a black sea of shock, fierce regret and searing pain.

I was supposed to be holding her hand when she died, sitting right beside her as I had been for the two-year lead-up to this dreaded moment. I was supposed to companion her to the very edge of the veil. I was supposed to have some kind of transcendent experience as solemn consolation from the gods for their taking her.

"Jac's the one accompanying my soul through this," she'd said to a friend, only weeks before. Fitting. This had been the nature of our bond since her body gave birth to mine, since her wholehearted love stitched the deep foundations of my being together. For 41 years that bond had been as vital to me as Life Itself.

Inconceivable, unforgiveable, that I'm not there.

"I'm sorry Mum, I'm so sorry."

Rocking on the floor, tears choke my breath as my fingers trace her freckled hands on the tiny screen of my phone. Lying still on her breathless chest, those hands are the symbol of my maternal line, and I ache to be touched by them one last time. Incomprehension fuels my disbelief, while the wild tearing in my chest plainly bares the truth of death in that parallel room.

Disintegration begins within me and I have no desire to stop it. Everything is wrong. Betrayal and shame swirl through my veins. We were supposed to have weeks. I was only gone four days.

My body heaves and I fall, winded, untethered from She who made me and the Love that anchored me. Motherless.

Time passes. Waves of heartbreak continue to build and crash through my limp body and I surrender to its cruel comfort. Those dogged parts of me that have worked solidly through this long dark night of cancer finally collapse. Not a scrap of fight left and the enemy just vanished into thin air. How I wish I could too.

And then, slowly, something yields in me, and I remember the lake. I remember the heart in the water, and I remember my words ... *If you need to let go, you can let go. I'm here* ... and I realise that she has, and her soul is now free. She is unbridled from the reins of space and time that I am still wildly railing against. And it dawns on me that I, too, am free – free from the cold confines of the hospital room, free from expectation and the dictates of clinical procedure. I am simply Here, and she is on her way There.

And so I take a candle and walk barefoot to the top of the grassy knoll. I stand still, alive and awake to her beautiful, pure essence. Earth, Water, Star and Air stand vigil with me as she slips from the fabric of our realm and takes up with the angels. Seamless. Beautiful even.

In the stillness, deep inside the raw ache of her absence, I think I detect the quiet hum of her presence. And for a breath, in this timeless time, this liminal space, I know I am not alone. And I know I am exactly where I need to be.

GRANDMA'S GIFT
by Kate Foulds

Lizzie self-consciously shoved a hand under her armpit as she approached the Hospital Street Flats.

Her school dress was stained with sweat and her face was sure to be as red as the ruby red lipstick Grandma stored in her fridge right beside the glad-wrapped ox-tongue.

It was the same routine every Friday.

Lizzie's mother would head into town to begin the weekly shop about 3.30pm.

While she walked and talked the aisles of Randall's IGA, before popping into Pete's fruit and veg and Gilly the butchers in readiness for the Sunday roast, Lizzie dragged her feet down to Grandma's for afternoon tea.

It was a change from catching the bus home from school but she would rather be at the pool with her friends.

As Lizzie approached the fly-wire door she stretched her arm towards the handle to find it turning of its own accord.

"Elizabeth, come along, the tea will be ruined."

One day Lizzie had asked her Grandmother why she insisted on calling her Elizabeth. She was told that, in their early married days, Grandpa had a cow called

Lizzie. "Every time your mother calls out to you it sounds like she's herding up dairy cows," she said.

And as far as Grandma was concerned, that was the end of the matter.

Lizzie took her place at the little corner table, which as usual was covered by the freshly-starched cloth dotted with colorful hand-embroidered daisies and Royal Albert china.

Grandma leaned over to pour what her father referred to with a roll of the eyes as "scented tea" but all Lizzie could smell was the lotion from Friday's ritual rinse and set at the hairdressers.

This was soon replaced by the aroma of freshly baked cream-puffs with lashings of award-winning strawberry jam and clotted cream.

Before Lizzie had a chance to smile in appreciation Grandma was settling back into her rocking chair, powdering her perfectly manicured if rather wrinkly hands, to resume her knitting.

As Lizzie sat and ate the delicious cake and endured the "scented tea", the only sound that broke the silence was the 'tick, tick, tick' of the little golden clock that sat on the telly, the rhythmic rock of Grandma's chair and the click, clack of knitting needles.

Grandma was focused only on the task before her. Lizzie sat and stared at her Grandmother's smooth stockings, royal blue tailored skirt suit and perfectly applied make-up.

“You-hoo,” her mother called from the door.

“I won’t come in, got to get the frozen food home out of this heat.”

Grandma put her knitting down and got up, but she didn’t say goodbye — she simply handed Lizzie an old book held together by a lacker band.

~

Grandma died on her 88th birthday.

Auntie Rena had arrived to take her out to lunch and found her sitting in her rocking chair all dressed up ready to go out.

Later that week, as Lizzie sat dry-eyed staring into the stained-glass windows of the church, she thought Grandma would have been happy to reach the gates of heaven with her ruby red lipstick on.

~

One evening after the kids were tucked into bed Lizzie resisted the temptation to flop onto the couch in front of the telly.

Now the extension was finished she was determined to get some of those old boxes in the shed sorted out.

As she leafed through a pile of books she stumbled across the tatty green one which had been handed to her many years before, with “My Recipe Book” on the faded cover.

The perished rubber band snapped in half before Lizzie could take it off and the book fell apart before her. Gathering up pages, she picked up the cover, and turned it over to read, "Presented to Miss E. Young 18/9/1927".

Who had presented the book to her maiden Grandma, and for what occasion?

Inside the book were recipes for Grandma's favourite home-baked treats and Lizzie was taken back to those silent Friday afternoons in Hospital Street.

Scattered among CWA recipes were hand-written knitting patterns with titles such as "Bryan's Knitted Trousers" and "Merle's Pull-over".

As she read on, Lizzie saw a much younger version of herself ripping into the brown paper package she would receive every birthday, only to feel her shoulders drop as she unfolded yet another hand-knitted cardigan.

As Lizzie lost herself in the pages she found recipe after recipe for Trout Amandine, Braised Trout, Baked Trout, Rabbit Casserole and Savoury Rabbits. She remembered lazy summer evenings fly-fishing at the Res. after setting rabbit traps on Wheeler's Hill with her father.

Among the pages scattered before her on the floor, there were newspaper clippings with lists of ingredients to concoct everything from furniture polish and hand lotion to quince jelly and blackberry jam. There was also the recipe for the "Special Rich Christmas Pudding" Grandma would bring as a peace offering to her mother's Christmas table each year.

The last recipe she found before the letters turned into a teary blur was for the choux pastry she mixed up on the stove-top with her mother as a little girl to make chocolate eclairs for the annual Show.

Lizzie covered her ears, for there was her Grandma's voice echoing through the room: "Elizabeth, I cook from the heart".

FRAUGHT & COMPLICATED

by Benjamin MacEllen

Mother.

I honestly can't think of a topic I'd rather not write about, except maybe Father. You see, I hate Mother's Day. I dread Mother's Day. And for the few days leading up to it, I avoid it as best I can. If I could sleep my way through from early to mid-May, I probably would.

I was born on Mother's Day 1970. As a result, my date of birth was not really my own for most of my life. My mother holds a strong claim to my birthday: the gift she got for Mother's Day 1970 was me. And from that day to this, Mother's Day and my birthday have been inextricably connected. Enmeshed. As if it's not enough to face the prospect of turning 50 this year (where did that time go?) I'm going to once again share my natal day with Mother's Day, only the seventh time Mother's Day has coincided with my birth date, or vice versa, but it's truly the gift that keeps on giving, every single year. It took 35 years to be able to claim my special day as my own. And even at 49, I'm still untangling mother from child.

Mother's Day for me means betrayal. The betrayal of a mother's love and protection for her child. They are the most fundamental qualities we celebrate and laud about mothers … their love, their unconditional love, and that they protect their children. How often have you heard a parent say, "I'd do anything for my kids" or "I'd die for my children!"? But it seems for some mothers there are more important things than love for a child.

I grew up in a middle-class home with everything, when it comes to practical needs, that I could ever want. The youngest of four children, I lived with my family in nice houses, my parents drove reliable cars, I went to good schools, we celebrated birthdays and Christmases, and all enjoyed fine health. In terms of possessions we weren't the richest, but I had toys, games, electronics and musical instruments. My mother was a good cook, and both my parents worked. My father held a position of moral importance, and both my parents concerned themselves with their status and standing in the community.

My partner, Darren, had a slightly less prosperous upbringing. He was the third of four children living on the poverty line in government housing. Despite financial hardship and his father's poor health, his parents remained together as he grew up. There was always food on the table at mealtimes and his mother would make clothes for him and his siblings.

In 1965, the year Darren was born, two elderly women knocked on the door of the family home. His mother Eve answered the door. Since the Cuban missile crisis in

1962, the world had been gripped with an existential fear of nuclear war. Eve was pregnant with Darren and had two young daughters to worry about. When the women asked her if she wanted to live forever in paradise on earth, she was suddenly faced with a solution to her fears beyond the fall-out shelter that the growing family could not afford. If she could live forever in paradise, she wouldn't need a doomsday plan. So, the naïve and vulnerable Eve took the two women's literature and joined a cult. A cult that provided community and fellowship with kindred folk, a guarantee of salvation and eternal life, but, well, there's the cultish part. Isolation from non-cult members; strict rules about acceptable and unacceptable behaviour; and the threat of demons and being separated from God.

Eve devoted her own life, and gradually the lives of her children and husband, 100% to that cult. It was like she sat down at a poker machine – being told that it was assured to pay out – and she kept putting in coins. She was totally invested in the pay out, that promise of paradise, and she couldn't step away. So, when it turned out that her eldest son Darren was something that was contrary to the beliefs of the cult, she believed she had no choice. She followed the instructions of the cult and rejected her son. One day he was part of a tight community of kinfolk, the next he was disowned, discarded, persona non grata. The love and acceptance he had enjoyed for twenty-one years of his life suddenly became disdain and disapproval. The friends and family that he loved and who had loved him now treated him like a stranger, crossing the road from where he walked. The only community he knew cast him out.

Darren did nothing wrong, and yet his mother rejected and abandoned him.

In my family, there were signs of gaslighting, psychological and verbal abuse long before the sexual abuse came to light. And my mother always excused it. It made me feel, like many victims/survivors of abuse, that I was to blame, or worse, that I was imagining it. When she chose to defend him, she didn't choose me. When a mother denies that abuse was perpetrated on a child, it breaks trust. It breaks that child's spirit. As a child I had no power and no voice to speak up, but I realised as an adult I could protect myself and walk away from my abusers and their toxic behaviour.

As I write this, I once again reflect on the experiences that my partner and I have had with our mothers. And it suddenly hits me: the irony of our mothers' similarity is that my mother invested in a man with a God complex, while Darren's mother just invested in something she believed to be 'God'. They refused to divest from the manipulation of men in power – ignoring all common-sense and every natural maternal instinct – and failed to love, nurture and protect their children.

Some people think that I'm a terrible, hateful, selfish child towards my mother. But I can't agree. I'm just a survivor who's unwilling to pretend it's all okay. She may honestly believe she did nothing wrong, even if by inaction or omission. I hope that gives her comfort in her final years. But on Mother's Day, and for the rest of my life, I will be working hard to heal the brokenness; the damage done by a mother who didn't believe me, who didn't protect me, and who didn't choose me.

It's a heart-breaking story, but hardly unique, when an adult child is estranged from their parent. In my case, it was ultimately my choice for my mental health. For my partner, Darren, the estrangement was forced upon him. I know some mothers and children who cringe at my intervention. They had healthy, loving, and strong relationships between parent and child, and can't quite imagine any circumstance that would tear that bond apart. Many have lost their mum over the years, and some more recently. Others, who are mums themselves, have buried children — something a parent should never have to do. They hold on tight to the ideal of a good mother/child relationship, and perhaps rightly feel aggrieved that any child would choose to sever the connection with their mum. But for every person who is uncomfortable with my decision to step away from my mother I ask: sit with that feeling, meditate on it, but please don't project it onto me and my personal history. Don't expect that to be my experience; it is simply not.

I pay tribute to all the mothers in my life who have been strong, protective, nurturing women, who have tried their best to love their children unconditionally. Goodness knows parenting is bloody difficult and try as we might we often make mistakes. Here's to the mums that made it work despite the mistakes; to those mums who have faced and continue to deal with great sadness at this time of year. To those mums who, despite their best efforts, are apart from their children on Mother's Day, I wish you love and healing.

To those children and grandchildren who are missing a special woman in their lives — I hope you are all comforted by the memories of happier times, and of Mother's Days past. To those children, young and old, who have sadness, resentment, or disquiet in their minds and hearts on Mother's Day, I say this: We are not defined solely by the relationships with our mothers. In spite of the hurts we suffered and continue to endure, we can learn to give ourselves the love, nurturing and acceptance our mothers failed to. We can not only survive the dark days, we can create new traditions, new connections, and new memories — with or without our mothers.

LIKE MOTHER, LIKE DAUGHTER

by Sophie Hay

Not so long ago, I said to my mother, "Remember when we were young, and we would spend the day at home playing café?"

We would hunt through the pantry and freezer, write up a menu with our discoveries and spend hours getting our café setting just right. Tablecloth, a small vase with the fresh seaside daisies that were always present but exploded in our front garden each summer. Even now, those daisies make me smile. They're so reminiscent of home.

We'd welcome our most loyal customer and serve her regular cup of tea with milk and sugar, ask what she would like to eat and busy ourselves creating a meal. A fruit platter for the best customer in town? Of course! Two party pies with sauce and a teaspoon to scoop out the meat? Coming right up! Those days, that game, the memory is just wrapped in love.

When I shared how special that memory is with Mum, she looked at me for a moment and said, "Those games, those days – we had nothing. We couldn't go anywhere, pay to do anything because we had no money. I was home, all the time, with four daughters.

Those games were out of necessity."

Perspective. It's a wonderful thing. How someone else's hard times can be some of your best memories.

We often hear that it's not about the things our parents give us, but the experiences. For us, that was unequivocally true. Mum gave us games, fanciful ideas, memorable experiences, belief in magic and whimsy, adventure. Waking up in the morning and running out to check our carefully constructed fairy garden only to discover there was water splashed from the seashell pool, the crumbs of the picnic scattered over the miniscule table, and one tiny shoe left behind. Oh, the excitement and joy we felt. I never want to lose that feeling, that joy in magical belief. Mum understood how much that meant to us.

The most valuable thing Mum ever gave us was a belief in ourselves. Not once in our lives have any of us felt as though we were unable to do exactly what it was we wanted to do. We were given everything we needed to be successful – emotional support, encouragement, a taxi, a shoulder to cry on. We were given a mother who was so committed to ensuring her four beloved daughters were always striving to be the greatest versions of themselves.

My mother is a teacher. A wonderful, passionate, dedicated teacher. A teacher who gives all of herself to her job, her kids, her colleagues and her school. A teacher who showed her daughters the importance of education, of knowledge and of building other people up. Just as importantly, she showed us the importance of being kind, and understanding that everyone is worthy of compassion and kind words. Mum understands the value of a quick smile, or a quiet touch on the shoulder to check if someone is ok. These small acts and gentle reminders were ubiquitous as we moved through our childhood, whether Mum realised we were noticing or not. Quietly observing our mother exist and grow in her profession has undoubtedly helped shape the way my sisters and I engaged in life, interacted with others, and generally saw the world. Mum inspired me so much I became a teacher myself, and I attempt to emulate her caring and committed nature daily.

One of the great joys in my adult life has been getting to know my mother as an equal, a friend, a woman who has an identity separate from 'mother'. She is a wonderful person. Mum is fun, she is curious, she is always pushing herself to do more. She is quick to a laugh. She loves to learn. She enjoys a mystery more than anyone I know. She loves a dance floor. I'm beginning to appreciate how similar I am to my mother, and for that I am thankful. Everything that forms my identity I can trace back to Mum. A love of books and stories, commitment to family, undeniable love of champagne. What fun we have sharing a glass of our much loved bubbles, not because we are obligated to spend time together, but because we truly enjoy each other's company.

Becoming a mother myself gave me a fresh perspective of how much you must give of yourself to your children, and how much that can change who you are as an individual. Mum has been ever patient with my constant stream of questions and wonderings, no matter how inane. "Is my child talking enough? When will she grow more hair? Should she be drinking more water? Is she going outside enough? Eating enough? ... am I enough?".

Our life is an ordinary one. Perfectly, wonderfully ordinary. We've found such happiness as a family, growing up in the ordinary. Growing up, branching out, creating our own families – but always coming back together whenever possible, our parents the beating heart and ever-present soul of the family.

My sisters and I are strong women, because a strong woman raised us. We are indisputably lucky to call Trish Johnstone our mother.

UNFORGETTABLE
by Jenny Mustey

I watched her hands grip the car door handle to steady herself, compose herself. I pulled into the servo on the highway and stopped the car. We hadn't made it far – just to the other side of the city. I heard her hold back the tears, she desperately didn't want to cry and let me see her crumble. We can go back mum, you don't have to do this, we can make it another time. No, she quietly reassures me, it will be ok, it was just that song – it was just too much, too soon. Let's keep going.

And kept going she has. Nearly 29 years have passed since that moment sitting in my old car heading to where my new home, where I still live today. We spoke quietly for the rest of the trip. It was hard and it was sad, both of us mulling over how and if we would get over our loss, our grief and our pain. We didn't want to say goodbye, no one ever does and it was still so hard to contemplate that dad had gone. He was only 55 and his new life as a retiree had only just begun. I was so crestfallen for Mum. All those shared plans and dreams were now never to be. We were all devastated and bewildered and our faith was challenged; for me this is still a personal struggle. But we have learnt to be brave and strong and we have Mum to thank for this.

She has been a pillar of strength. I would be naïve to say that it's all been easy and I have no doubt there have been many moments of silent fury, anger and despair but her strong faith continues to uphold her and she has surrounded herself with good, wise and loving people who share a similar spiritual and philosophical approach to life.

I strongly suspect she has always made a promise to herself to get on with things and embrace what comes her way. We have seen her turn 60, then 70 and then a radiant 80. She has worked, she has travelled overseas, she has cared for grandchildren, she has enjoyed live theatre, trips to the football, musicals and movies and embraced technology – surprising herself along the way. She has kept active, creative and centred and often says "how could a person be bored?". I have watched her juggle a number of commitments and tasks and I am totally in awe of the passionate, selfless way she contributes her time and energy to ensure others feel supported and loved. Her weeks are full of busy things and a great sense of family and community connection.

Our phone calls over the years have played a significant part in maintaining our enduring relationship. She has shared my joy, my fears, my triumphs and I have received so much in return. Her words of encouragement down the line have never failed to move me and her description of her week reassures me that things are still ok. I love hearing her say, "It's been such a busy week", which means our conversation becomes full of the comings and goings of family and friends, book club, home group, exercises, medical appointments, shopping expeditions, Probus outings and sadly more recently the funerals of friends she has now lost. Still she goes on.

My experience is different to my brother and sister; mine has been from a distance over the last 29 years but I still feel that same loving connection to her as they do. Perhaps that distance made it stronger. We value and treasure those times when we see each other. We have enjoyed delightful catch-ups in the city for lunch. We've talked into the early hours when I have popped down to stay for a night or two. We can sit at the dining table for hours and just prattle on about random topics. We have been to concerts, exhibitions and we have shared our love of reading, British crime shows and binged Netflix shows together. Over the years she has visited me many times and usually stays a few days at a time, sometimes just to look on into our world or it might be for a significant work event or family celebration or to touch base with the grandchildren. It doesn't matter the reason, I have valued and appreciated every time she has made the journey to be with me.

Mum, I admire and respect how you have not dwelt

on sadness and the emptiness you no doubt often feel but have remained self-assured and true to yourself and to all those around you.

Looking back at that unforgettable day in 1991, I thank you for reassuring me that you would be ok – and you have continued to show me how.

CUMIN, TURMERIC, CORIANDER

by Shobie Owen

On wintry mornings, crouching on the heating vent behind her flowing batik sarong

The aroma of sizzling of spices soaking into our hair as we rush out the door for school

Frantic sprays of perfume on our heads in an attempt to hide the smell from our Aussie classmates

Running home to a predictable, soothing pot of sambar, dried fish and steaming rice

Cumin, turmeric, coriander

Please do your false teeth trick Paati, we plead, as sambar drips down our chins

You willingly oblige, making us all laugh and shriek with delight

We poke and prod at your papery skin, smoothing it as though it were fabric

And marvel at the gold bangles that encircle your plump forearms

Secretly, we borrow your shiny saris for our childhood games

We plaster our foreheads with your bindis and adorn our necks with your 24-carat gold wedding thaali
We take turns imagining that we are the resplendent brides meeting our husbands on our wedding day for the very first time

You regale us with tales of a foreign land and a distant time
We pull at your elbow and examine the scars on your legs and beg for the wounded soldier story once more
You speak of the jungles that were your backyard
And the tropical trees dripping with more juicy fruit than you could ever desire

Mango, papaya, durian, tiger balm

The thud of the mortar and pestle rhythmically crushing, smashing, bringing ginger and garlic to life
The loud cacophony of Tamil films taunts me from my bedroom desk and I give in, forsaking my homework to sit at your feet
A quiet soprano of Indian songs escapes your open lips, but you're not a performer so we must come in close to hear you sing barely audibly, as you de-seed dried chili with turmeric-stained fingers

Regular sojourns to your homeland
Excitement builds as we collect you from the airport

waiting for you to peel open your suitcase and reveal Malaysian delights

No sooner than the spices are unpacked, you are soaking the tamarind ready to squeeze its juice into a big fat pot of rassam

Tamarind, chili, cardamon, garam masala

Crisply-ironed Kanchipuram silk saris of all varieties adorn you for weddings, deaths and graduations

Fresh black henna makes your crown shine, yet your drooping shoulders carry the weight of lost children

Death brings chaos and colour into my western brick veneer home: Tamil music, garlands, dead bodies, food, community

Formidable Women, my flesh and blood, beating their chests and wailing as they keep watch

You are the centre of the menu planning which begins weeks in advance for any gathering of the clan ... your absolute favourite pastime

From your chair, you see it all

You know the details of the flowers in the garden as intimately as the contents of the fridge

Mentally sorting which morsel gets assigned to which mouth so that there will be enough for everyone

But you will always eat last

Sambal, acar, biriani, lamb curry

Who would I be without these sights, smells, sounds and experiences?

Dearest Paati, my cultural saviour in this foreign land, my warm and loving grandmother, whose presence is woven through the fabric of our lives.

LACUNA
by Pam Harvey

Spring 2006

My mother – a small, rounded woman of 81 – picks up her car keys and goes to leave for home, fifteen minutes drive away. "Don't forget this," I say, pulling a blue jacket from the back of a chair and handing it to her.

"That's not mine," she says.

I remember her looping it over the solid wooden chair. "I think it is."

"No," says Mum. "That is not my jacket."

We stand in the kitchen staring at the benign navy fleece. In the background, my two children watch television. It has been a weekend of visitors. I am tired. The house is a mess. I must get ready for the week ahead.

"This is the jacket that you came in with," I say, giving it a little shake.

Mum's face hardens. "This is not my jacket. *She* must've taken mine."

She clearly doesn't mean me. It could only mean my friend who is driving back interstate as we speak. I don't think *she* would have taken the wrong jacket but how could I be sure? "I'll give her a ring later."

Mum leaves, sans jacket. I ring my friend. "No," she says. "Not mine."

I drop in on Mum after work the next day. "You must have picked up the wrong jacket at church."

"I did not." Mum's ginger eyes are unusually glittery. "*She* has taken my jacket."

I leave the jacket on the spare bed. It is dark on the white bedspread. I can't help thinking it is gathering a black-hole kind of darkness that it had not possessed before.

A week goes by. "I miss that jacket," Mum says on the phone every night. "I have nothing to wear."

"Well," I say. "What about you wear the blue jacket on the spare bed? We aren't sure whose it is so you might as well use it."

There is a brief silence. "I am not wearing that jacket. I want my own back."

On Friday, I duck out of work to the shop where Mum buys her clothes and get her a new navy-blue jacket. I drive to her place and present it. Mum takes it automatically then flings it down on the bed. "I think it's a very cruel thing that she's done, stealing a jacket from an old lady like me. It's absolutely disgraceful."

Blood hurts my ears. I take both jackets away.

Another week goes by. The silence is blessed but puzzling. The jackets have been forgotten.

Summer 2008

Mum is referred to The Memory Clinic, an ominous-sounding place (are memories lost or found there?). Our first appointment is with a nurse and a social worker who visit Mum's house. We have separate interviews. I feel like a dobber as I describe Mum dressed up ready to go to a concert that doesn't exist, her forgetfulness in the supermarket and her confabulation of daily activities that haven't happened.

After half an hour, the nurse who has been seeing Mum in the kitchen comes into the lounge room to where I sit with the social worker. "I've left your mother in there with a few pamphlets," she says.

What pamphlets?

"Symptoms of dementia. I think she has Alzheimer's."

I'm horrified.

Firstly, that Mum would have been left alone with a brochure broadcasting dementia; and, secondly, I don't want to hear these words. I'm not ready for dementia either in a pamphlet or in real life. I don't want my mother to forget me.

Autumn 2012

Mum's diagnosis is not Alzheimer's but vascular dementia, a sawtooth progression of loss and plateau, loss and plateau. She goes to live in a residential care facility. Within weeks, she gains two dress sizes and recovers her happy, social life.

"I'm not so good today," Mum says occasionally and touches her head lightly. Or: "I'm getting very wooden.

I have holes where memories used to be."

I visit one day to see her favourite olive green jacket – faded, pilled, soft – stretched neatly out on her bed. "This is not my jacket," she says but the tone is resigned, as weary as the loved item in front of us.

"It is," I say gently. "It even has your name on it."

She rubs at the laundry label, one of many ironed to every item of clothing she has. I wonder in that moment whether she recognizes her name so we just stand and stare at the jacket as if it could be replenished from its ageing state with the power of our gaze. After a while, I put it back on its hanger and set it into the wardrobe. Mum doesn't stop me. Her sadness makes my throat tighten.

I imagine a brain disconnecting and neural pathways interrupted, grey matter patchy with plaques and fibrous with tangles. Poetically, the presence of multiple brain lesions in dementia is a 'lacuna state'. Lacuna, from the Latin meaning pit or gap. Thoughts disappear, memories can't form. How strange and discombobulating it would be to fall down that hole.

Winter 2014

Two years of snail-paced decline but it isn't dementia that takes her. On Friday, she eats lunch with her four children around her. She smiles at us, pats my hand, and closes her eyes.

We sit at her bedside, my brothers and me, and swap stories of our childhoods; of tuna casseroles and dogs and running under the hose on scorching summer days. We talk about Mum's beauty at 18, of getting her licence at 55, of becoming a widow at 70. We laugh a lot, sob a bit, take turns to buy rubbishy take-away fried chicken. It's a glittering gem of time. I'm positive Mum hears us.

On Monday evening, with my turn at the chicken shop, she goes quietly.

Spring 2019

We are sorting photos and scanning them in pre-fire season preparation. There's Mum, a whole gamut of images. A baby held by Grandma, a young woman in war-time, a bride in a dress made from satin collected with donated ration cards. She is always smiling; a broad, bright-eyed direct gaze at the camera.

The opposite of lacuna is fullness, wholeness, entirety.

I think of Mum often because mothers never really leave you. Mine filled me up with love. The lacunae, well, they've long disappeared.

PAT'S PLACE
by Shann Lions

Mothers have an innate way of expressing their love.

As a child, my mother sometimes grabbed my arms and pulled me in so tightly that I struggled to breathe. I would turn my head to the side so I didn't drown in the abundance of my mother's affection — and mostly I tried to avoid it. It was how she communicated her love for me.

For everyone else, my mother would communicate her love through food.

During my childhood in the 1980s, my mother cooked in pubs. My parents later bought a shop in Rushworth, Victoria, and we lived both there, in a house behind the shop, and on a farm midway between Cooma and Stanhope.

The shop was known as 'Pat's Place'. Mum cooked for the townsfolk and for tourists who were bused in to check out the local Aboriginal watering holes, the ghost-filled cemetery, and an open-cut gold mine in the Whroo state forest.

In Pat's Place, I learnt compassion for others by observing my mother utilising her cooking skills as a conduit to communicate with people.

As a seven-year-old, I remember one of the town's more colourful characters coming into Pat's Place to have Christmas lunch with Mum. He didn't rush, staying for more than an hour to enjoy every morsel — and her company.

Moments like these, normal at the time and not overly appreciated through a child's eyes, taught me values.

Mum would play music while she cooked. To this day, artists such as Jose Carreras, Stevie Wonder, The Eagles, and Billy Ocean trigger thoughts of the culinary items emanating from her inner sanctum — chocolate chip cookies, fried rice, cannelloni, and the pumpkin soup that famously ended up being featured in *The Weekly Times Cook Book*.

The Eagles are the only one of those acts I enjoy listening to as an adult. I didn't pick up my mother's cooking ability, either. I'd much rather write a song than bake a scone.

My ability to write and perform music comes through my father's lineage. Waka, as he's known around the traps, is still playing in the same concert band after 25 years. He has an early 1980s boom box in his workshop that is still going strong, with classics such as Jimi Hendrix, The Who, Dire Straits, and obscure blues artists blasting from its tinny speakers.

I have a tattoo of that boom box on my arm as a tribute to the resilience of an inanimate object, my childhood, and, in a roundabout way, our family.

It is my mother who connects me to my adopted hometown of Bendigo; she was born here and grew up in the suburb of White Hills. And it was her ties to this golden town that prompted me to make my own move here.

Back in 1997, I might as well have been contemplating residing in New York City. I was living in Carag Carag, a tiny town with a population of just 35. By day I worked on a tomato farm in nearby Corop, playing a guitar in my downtime.

But I knew I had a soft place to land in Bendigo, so I packed my car and drove down the highway. I set myself up in a caravan at my aunt and uncle's house in Strathfieldsaye.

I told my parents I would get an education, but the only learning I did was playing rock and roll on stage.

I am a sub-par cook, and I'm OK with that. I wouldn't want to encroach on my mother's purple patch of culinary skills. I spend all my spare time writing songs — not using tongs. But one day I may learn some of her recipes before it's too late.

As I grow older, at times I reflect on how my mother has directly and subconsciously shaped elements of the path I am now walking. All these years later, she is still holding my hand along life's journey, and I remain grateful for that.

THE LEGACY
by Jenny Mitchell

If we're lucky our mothers instil in us values, ideas, pleasures and ways of being that will be helpful to us as we navigate our way through life.

I am one of the lucky ones and, while it's hard to know how far back to go, my own mother was lucky enough to have a mother who valued education. And who, uneducated herself, took in laundry so that she could send her daughter to private school and to university at a time when this was not the norm.

Thus my mother learned to love stories, reading, words and knowledge. On long family trips she became our very own audio book, introducing us to forever favourites like *My Family and Other Animals*. So many ideas, events and names for things made their way into our lives from the books that were read to us — including our much loved little sailing boat, Bootle Bumtrinket.

Apparently it was Albert Einstein who said that if you want your kids to be intelligent read them fairy tales and if you want them to be more intelligent read them more fairy tales. I doubt my mother ever heard this but her own classical education meant that she valued fairy tales as well as myths and legends and she passed that love onto us. We had books and books of fairy tales from all around the world as well as piles of Puffin books for Christmas and birthdays. My mother was always reading — always. I am always reading — always with a book close at hand.

My mother loved an adventure.

In 1948, when she was only 21 she travelled from Adelaide to Perth, then up the west coast and over the seas to Borneo. She had married eight months before but hadn't been allowed to accompany dad to his first job. Borneo wasn't considered safe for a new bride or maybe the company didn't want dad to be distracted while he settled into his work. Like so many women of that era she went straight from daughter living at home to wife running a home — in her case a grass hut with the threat of skink tails falling from the timber beams into the soup and the fear of being blasted across the room, eyebrows singed, because of an unstable gas supply to the oven.

There were trips up river to the Dayak tribal gatherings, a pet monkey and crazy attempts to surf with the wooden ironing board.

My mother was unconventional.

She was an early feminist with a great sense of fun and who was frustrated by the strictures of her time.

Her sense of social justice was well-developed. When she lived in South Africa she staged her own anti-apartheid protest in the local shop by insisting that the Zulu women, who would usually have to wait until all the white women were served, be attended to before her. She paid bills for a family whose father had lost his job and helped a young Turkish girl escape from an abusive family situation. Is it any wonder I became a social worker?

My mother taught me to be brave.

She encouraged me to keep going to school when I was being bullied by my grade six teacher but promised to meet me at the school gate at the end of every day with open arms and words of comfort. She kept that promise until I told her that I had got to the point of being able to get home on my own without breaking down.

My mother was a Tidy Tessie.

When she reorganised my linen cupboard after my babies were born, I couldn't bear to undo such perfection so I recycled the linen and towels for months — washing and drying the same sets in one day. And even now when I reach into my linen cupboard I remember that kindness.

My mother was a Supergran.

It was lovely to see her with my girls. There were treats and treasures and books and beautiful knitted garments. There were circular skirts and bouncy balls and gentle walks around the block and in the great outdoors. It was wonderful to see and to be reminded of how well I had been loved and nurtured as a child.

My mother left a great legacy.

I learned to choose my own path and have faith in my ability to get there. I learned to accept others however different, to be kind, to protect and stick up for the underdog and to value education, stories, reading and knowledge. I learned to be thankful for and generous to friends and strangers.

When I think of my childhood I remember love, laughter and togetherness. When I think of the family I now live in I think of love, laughter and togetherness and I realise how lucky I am to have had a mother who instilled these things in me.

I am definitely one of the lucky ones.

IN RHONDA'S GARDEN
by Deb Wain

Even as a teenager, when such laments are rife, I never felt that my mother did not understand me. My fear was that she understood me too well, that we were too similar, and for this reason we clashed.

Some of the similarities are surface level: we look alike, have similar cheekbones, our eye and hair colours are the same. These, of course, aren't things that create problems or conflicts. It was more like our mutual stubbornness, our desire to be right, to have the last word. When we didn't agree, these traits created friction. What we did agree on was gardening. Even now, at 47 , I feel an enduring desire to mark myself out as my own person, but some things are deeply linked to my childhood and, in particular, to the garden my mother, Rhonda, grew then.

From the time when my parents married until I was about 12-years-old, we lived on a residential block in the outer western suburbs of Melbourne. The spaces were carved up plots of tired agricultural land with red clay soil that stained clothes and bent garden forks. On this patch of claret-coloured clay, my mother marked herself out as a gardener. The garden was Rhonda's domain.

Dad dug holes where she indicated he should dig. He didn't make the decisions. In a rebellious response to her own mother's cottage garden and annual colour that needed planting and re-placing, my mother went for native plants. She despised the stocks her mother grew. I don't know what stocks are and find myself checking the tags in the Bunnings garden department looking to identify the offending flora.

It started with a lemon-scented gum purchased at a local nursery. Its tag identified not only its species name – at the time, *Eucalyptus citriodora* – but also the fact that it had been grown by a native plant nursery called Australflora. Rhonda trekked out to the Dandenongs and visited the nursery itself; perhaps she was inspired by the healthy growth of the gum. It grew alongside one of the few non-native trees on the property: a claret ash. The ash was one of five trees included in the house and land package my parents had purchased. There was also a golden ash in the backyard and something lanky and sickly-looking in the middle of the front lawn that my dad complained about mowing around until they dug it out, allowing the grass to grow over the scar. The lemon-scented gum dwarfed the ash that stood as its neighbour on the other side of the carport, marking a blurry border between our quarter-acre and that of the neighbours.

That gum and the nursery trip that followed its purchase was the beginning of my mother's long-running relationship with Austraflora. The owner, one of the brothers who started the nursery, talked with Rhonda about the soil and the local climatic zone, offering tips on how to break up the red clay. He advised on plants that would suit. Mum and Dad subsequently rotary-hoed the garden beds, adding gypsum and stable straw that could still be sourced locally. Not all of the agricultural land had been given over to low-income housing estates; some paddocks had become horse agistment.

Rhonda was a skilled gardener. She made notes on what grew and what didn't. She was ruthless about cutting her losses if a plant, wasn't performing to her liking. We would later joke that her criticism, 'This thing is doing nothing here' and the resultant removal of the offending plant is what kept all of us on our toes.

One outstanding success was a grevillea planted in a space along the front path. The foliage was more effective than a guard dog at ensuring uninvited guests didn't arrived unannounced. Those navigating the path were routinely gouged by its needles and their hollers sounded their arrival. Those who knew gave it a wide berth. I liked its curlicued red flowers and was glad when Rhonda defended the plant against complaints. She was amused rather than apologetic.

Outside the window of the bedroom I shared with my two sisters grew a sprawling acacia that was perhaps too successful. It was removed thanks to its role in my middle sister's hayfever. At some time, it must have had companions within the garden it had taken over but, at the time of its removal, it was alone. Its demise created a space that I don't recall being filled very effectively before we sold the house. Outside of this garden, on the edge of the lawn and at another vague property boundary with our neighbours on the opposite side, grew a pittosporum. Its new foliage came in red before turning a glossy dark green. The dense leaves created a shady space that a girl could hide inside and fill a bucket with the pretty but dead bodies of dragonflies. Both Rhonda and I know now that pittosporums, although native, are generally considered weeds outside of their indigenous areas. Back then, it filled a space and blocked the view to the neighbour's front door.

When I was 12, we moved from the suburban block to a much larger gardening blank slate – four acres in Woodend. I hadn't known at the time how much my mother had wanted to regain some of the space she had grown up with on farms in regional Victoria, but I recognise now that her time in the suburbs must have been a compromise. The new block and the house we built there afforded me the opportunity of witnessing my mother in full gardening action. She was starting from scratch.

By this time, I had discovered an interest in the environment and was firmly behind Rhonda's previous policy of planting natives, so I was dismayed when she began bringing home rhododendrons, azaleas and camellias. She planted these alongside indigofera and amongst the straight trunks of the existing eucalypts, but I still felt betrayed. Just when I was getting interested in following her way, she'd veered off into unknown territory. When I asked her about this choice recently, she explained it had been purely pragmatic. She had a large space to fill, the local nurseries were pushing these species, and the plants grew well in the cooler and wetter climate at the base of Mt Macedon. She was also working fulltime with three teenaged daughters which didn't leave time for trips back to Austraflora to find out what would grow best in this new dark and crumbly soil that looked nothing like the baked terracotta of our previous home. I realise now that there wasn't any change in her approach; it was pragmatism that led her to natives, and a touch of rebellion against the gardens of her own mother, and it was the same practicalities that led her to broadening her scope.

I helped establish this new garden: digging holes, planting out, and watering in. But Rhonda still pointed out where things were to go. Before long, though, I left home to pursue my interest in the environment via a teaching degree in Environmental Studies. At university, I found that my early upbringing amongst native plants gave me an advantage over my classmates, especially when it came to subjects reliant on plant identification.

At home, on the four acres in Woodend, Mum's

garden continued to expand and to grow. It became home to daffodils, ornamental plums, and lavender planted alongside poas, hakeas and those trusty grevilleas. I loved coming home – I still do – to the fresh air, the space and the plants, even though I still had a preference for natives.

In the three houses where I've lived and gardened as an adult, I have followed my passion for flora that's at least native, if not indigenous to the locale. For a while, I edited the newsletter for our local indigenous plant nursery in Croydon, named for the majestic *Eucalyptus rubida*. We bought plants as tube stock from Candlebark Nursery when we removed the old garden and the lawn of our first home, a two-bedroom weatherboard in an established part of the suburb, to plant out our own little piece of native habitat. We dug out camellias, rhododendrons and azaleas.

I've spent much of my life trying to distinguish myself from my mother, to be who I am aside from her, but the fact remains: we are very alike. I even have a prickly grevillea growing along the path to my front door.

Author Biographies

Elizabeth Beck

Elizabeth Beck was born and educated in Bendigo. She graduated from Frankston Teachers College and later completed further Degrees in Education, ESL and Librarianship, and taught in Victoria, interstate and overseas in many and varied schools. Elizabeth has 3 adult children, an extensive productive garden, with her own beehive, and is involved in many community interests and projects.

Elizabeth's contribution to *Mother* is **Nancie Hesse Lund** on page 25.

Rodney Carter

Rodney Carter is a descendant of Dja Dja Wurrung people and currently works for his people as the Group Chief Executive Officer of the Dja Dja Wurrung Clans Aboriginal Corporation and the Dja Dja Wurrung Enterprises Pty Ltd. Rodney was a member of the Dja Dja Wurrung negotiation team that negotiated a native title settlement agreement with the State of Victoria over a period of three years. This resulted in his people signing a 'Recognition and Settlement Agreement' on the 24th October 2013 with the State of Victoria. He has also worked with the Victori-an Public Land Fire Management as a Heritage Specialist and is a recipient of the National Emergency Medal from the Black Saturday fires of 2009. He is currently the Chairperson of the Victorian Aboriginal Heritage Council, and a member of the state's Regional Partnerships Committee for the Loddon Campaspe area.

Rodney's contribution to *Mother* is **Fay Priscilla Carter** on page 9.

T.S.F.Dowling

T. S. F. Dowling is a Bendigo poet, performer, editor & teacher. Her words form in poetic nests, hatch and fly across Australia, the UK and USA to land in anthologies, readings and exhibits. Community, arts, social justice, nature and the past have inspired her work for over 25 years. Books include Memoirs of a Consenting Victim (Mark Time Books, 2011), and Butcher, Baker, His-Story Maker, a verse novel (Birdfish Books, 2020).

T.S.F.'s contribution to *Mother* is **Lines Of Blood & Water & Stone** on page 39.

Kate Foulds

Kate Foulds grew up on the family farm in Musk. She completed a post-graduate journalism cadetship at Kyneton's *Midland Express* before cultivating her craft at *The Bendigo Advertiser*. She was a public relations consultant before establishing a small business alongside her husband. Kate has had volunteer reading and writing roles with Vision Australia Radio, Bendigo Youth Choir and The Victorian Embroiderers Guild, plus part time council media officer work. Kate currently enjoys crochet and serving customers at a Bendigo boutique. She is mother to a son and daughters who are identical twins.

Kate's contribution to *Mother* is **Grandma's Gift** on page 63.

Pam Harvey

Pam Harvey lives in Mandurang South and also writes under the name of Juno Harvey. She has published short stories, children's fiction, and women's fiction, and regularly reviews books for ReadingTimeOnline. Her writing grants include a VicArts Creators grant and a May Gibbs Creative Fellowship. She writes in the cracks between working at her day job and being with her family.

Pam's contribution to *Mother* is **Lacuna** on page 95.

Sophie Hay

Sophie Hay grew up in Bendigo and after a few years away, moved home to be closer to her family. She is married to Clint and they have a one-year-old daughter, Della. Sophie is a kindergarten teacher and she loves nothing more than a good book.

Sophie's contribution to *Mother* is **Like Mother, Like Daughter** on page 77.

Helen Hickson

Dr. Helen Hickson is a social worker, researcher and writer with a long-standing interest in rural communities. Helen has worked internationally and presented her work at a range of national and international conferences. She has been writing for about 15 years, first academically and then publishing both fiction and non-fiction writing. Helen is based near Bendigo and finds rural communities to be fascinating places; rich with stories of interesting people, historical events, scandals and celebrations.

Helen's contribution to *Mother* is **The Art Of Knitting** on page 19.

Nat Jane

Nat Jane works in Media Communications, involving technical and creative writing. She is in the process of turning her recent research in to her first novel.

Nat's contribution to *Mother* is **A Modern Mother** on page 31.

Shann Lions

Shann Lions is a singer, songwriter and producer, who heads up the group, Four Lions and also runs Gold Roses 3550, an alt country music festival in Bendigo.

Shan's contribution to *Mother* is **Pat's Place** on page 101.

Benjamin MacEllen

Benjamin MacEllen is a memoirist, lyricist, poet and activist. He writes and speaks extensively about his experience as a transgender man which is also the focus of his memoir, *A Cut Closer to Whole*. He was a semi-finalist at the World Championship of Public Speaking in Chicago in 2018. In his speaking engagements he advocates for better understanding of LGBTIQ+ issues. Ben's one-man show, *Transmansplaining* was performed in 2019 in Bendigo and Castlemaine.

Benjamin's contribution to *Mother* is **Fraught & Complicated** on page 69.

Karen Lee Mills

Karen Lee Mills is a prize-winning author, best known for her poetry, short article publications and her children's picture book, *Precious Artwork*. Karen is a public speaker and presents author talks in schools and local writers groups. She resides in rural Victoria.

Karen's contribution to *Mother* is **No Royal Bloodlines** on page 36.

Jenny Mitchell

Jenny Mitchell is a Bendigo-based social worker, one of the foundation members of Bendigo Writers Festival and an avid reader.

Jenny's contribution to *Mother* is **The Legacy** on page 105.

Jenny Mustey

Jenny Mustey is surrounded by books every day. She moved to Echuca 34 years ago to take up a position as a Teacher Librarian and then moved over to local government in 1997 and has managed the Campaspe Regional Library for the past 16 years. Her love of reading was instilled from an early age and she is still an avid reader and more recently a reviewer of Australian Women's contempo-rary and historical fiction and has been involved in the Australian Women Writers Challenge over the last five years.

Jenny's contribution to *Mother* is **Unforgettable** on page 83.

Joan Strack O'Brien

Joan Strack O'Brien a mother to two Bendigo-born daughters, after moving here with her husband almost 15 years ago. She is an Architect and is passionate about community and connection. She is also an only child.

Joan's contribution to *Mother* is **Bloodlines** on page 56.

Shobie Owen

Shobie Owen is a second generation migrant of South Indian/Sri Lankan descent. She was raised in the northern suburbs of Melbourne by her parents who migrated in the 1970s shortly after the White Australia Policy was abolished. Though they had their own struggles against racism and connecting meaningfully to life in the west, they had a strong faith and were instrumental in teaching Shobie and her siblings about loving your neighbour, extending radical hospitality and pursuing justice. Shobie has lived and worked amongst culturally and linguistically diverse communities for many years including South America, South East Melbourne and Central Australia. She now resides in Central Victoria where she raises her three daughters and practises social work. Shobie has always been passionate about writing and particularly enjoys bringing to life the many facets, nuances and faces of her ethnically diverse existence in Australia.

Shobie's contribution to *Mother* is **Cumin, Turmeric, Coriander** on page 89.

Dawn Rasmussen

As a baby boomer, Dawn Rasmussen admits she can sign her name to several very different careers. One of the most cherished of them is as a journalist with Australian Community Media. She is also the author and publisher of two monthly children's magazines which are full of fun and wacky info for kids. As the eldest of eight siblings, she was nominated early on as the 'responsible' one and this has morphed into being the official negotiator for family feuds.

Dawn's contribution to *Mother* is **This Maven Was A Flipper** on page 13.

Jacqueline Anne Sheridan

Jacqueline Sheridan is a lover of Beauty and a Seeker in the ways of soul. She lives and works in Castlemaine, holding therapeutic space for individuals and groups, using the sweet power of words, deep imagination, creativity, and the mothering of Nature to support our journey towards health and wholeness. She is a novice writer and poet and is just pushing off into her wild adventure in these waters.

Jacqueline's contribution to *Mother* is **Here & There** on page 59.

Deb Wain

Deb Wain is a local creative writer of, mostly, short stories but she also dabbles in poetry. She lives, and writes, on acreage on Taungurung country being kept company by one human, five chooks, two dogs, many kangaroos and the occasional echidna or three.

Deb's contribution to *Mother* is **In Rhonda's Garden** on page 111.

www.ingramcontent.com/pod-product-compliance
Lightning Source LLC
Chambersburg PA
CBHW030644190726
48286CB00008B/2641

* 9 7 8 1 9 2 5 9 0 0 0 0 2 *